W9-DHY-966

Sharing
a Dream

by Glen Threlfo

© Copyright Glendon Threlfo 1985

Published in Australia by

ANZEA PUBLISHERS
3-5 Richmond Road
Homebush West, NSW 2140, Australia

and distributed by
UK: Scripture Union, London
USA: Scripture Union, Philadelphia
Sth Africa: SUPA, Capetown

National Library of Australia
Cataloguing-in-Publication data.
Threlfo, Glendon, 1945-.
  Sharing a dream.
ISBN 0 85892 265 7

  1. Natural history — Australia — Pictorial works.
  I. Title.

574.994

Printed by Singapore National Printers (Pte) Ltd.

DEDICATION

This book is dedicated to God the Designer,
the Creator and Life Giver.
All praise goes to Him.
It is beyond the capacity of man to create
a living creature of his own design.
But we have been given an intelligent,
appreciative mind so that we can look with wonderment,
and praise God for everything around us.

INTRODUCTION

Australia abounds with unique and beautiful creatures. My intrigue with our wild life heritage developed rapidly after I was given a nature book at Secondary School. Ronald K. Monro produced magnificent work, with stories and beautiful photographs of birds and animals raising their young. It captured my interest and imagination with its entertainment and humour. His work has enriched my life and stimulated my love of nature. I find it sad to see a child who once showed interest in a lizard, a bird or a tiny flower turn purely to material things and artificial productions for entertainment.

It has been my dream to share with both adults and children some of the magical moments experienced in the hills and plains of our beautiful country. Photography is a wonderful means of capturing highlights of life and sharing them far and wide with others.

The good times roaming hills and streams would not have been the same without two friends who have been great company while giving great encouragement. Peter Pritchard shared five years of his life with me and his fascination for all the denizens of the bush has left an indelible impression on my mind.

Special thanks to Jon Brinsmead of Tweed Heads, a keen observer with an incredible talent to spot birds and their nests; also to Paul White who helped with the script.

Lotus Birds, also called Comb-crested Jacana, are among Australia's most delicate and beautiful birds. They are found only on the swamps and lagoons of northern Australia and down the east coast of Queensland and northern New South Wales. Their habit of skipping from water lily leaf to water lily leaf has gained for them the name Lily-trotter.

Lotus Birds are elegant, almost oriental, with their necks ornamented with soft gold and yellow. The comb changes colour in keeping with the bird's emotions. Excellent weight distribution comes from long green legs and exceptionally long toes. There is a ballet quality about their movement across the floating lily leaves. Being small and not easily seen in their environment, they are not frequently observed and many Australians do not know of their existence.

Lotus Bird is one of the few birds in the world who carries the newly hatched chicks under the wings as it skips across the lily leaves. As far as is known this study is the first record

On a stage of green leaves and encircled by colourful water lilies, Lotus Bird stretches out a leg and a wing and soaks up sunlight. This intimate study of Lotus Bird life was made possible by Glen Threlfo's vast patience and his ingenious prefabricated hides.

A storm strikes the lagoon. Lotus Bird's nest is torn apart and swept away. The hen is deeply concerned and the colour of her comb changes. She chooses a new nest site where her black and gold eggs, decorated with tar-like scribbles, will be safe. The shell is coated with a shiny, protective, waterproof layer since, from time to time, the eggs are partly submerged as the hen sits to incubate.

The hen has found a new site for her nest. She stands proudly upright, declaring this to be her new home.

Dragging long reeds across the leaves was no easy task, but, the work completed, back she comes to her eggs and makes her next incredible move.

She rolls the eggs off the damaged nest and sends them bobbing through the water. Most eggs would sink but those of the Lotus Bird float. The hen runs to her new nesting site and scoops each egg onto the lily leaves.

Many naturalists believe birds cannot count, but mother Lotus Bird knew one egg was missing so she searches under the edges of the leaves. Having found the lost egg she carefully rolls it to the new nesting place. She works hard reconstructing her nest and after four hours she again settled gently over her precious eggs.

After so many hours in the cold water it was wonderful to see the eggs crack open and the miracle of three small chicks emerging into the warmth of the sunny morning.

The little fellows take their first peep at the world around them and watch the last chick come out of his shell.

He looks up at his mates and down at his long thin toes.

Within minutes of hatching they move onto the lily leaves, staggering and tripping over as they try out their oversized feet. The two half-dried chicks discuss the weak and sticky latest arrival into the family.

Then they give their newly hatched brother a warm welcome. We all like a little attention and littlest Lotus Bird thinks it's great to feel part of the family.

Mother calls them
back to the nest and
opens her wings
slightly, encouraging
them to nestle under
her. One chick is
standing on her
long toes.

Two chicks have pushed up between the primary feathers of her right wing and the other is under the left wing.

She rises and with one big step carries her brood with her across the leaves with six legs and twenty-four toes dangling from her wings.

Three fluffy Lotus Birds spend their first morning drying in the sunlight and looking at the beautiful surroundings. One chick notices her brother's feet and studies them intently. The chicks confer seriously about the subject.

Young Lotus Bird, only 5cm tall, is a gem of beauty. He poses proudly and stretches the scrap of bone and skin that is his wing — the wing which will later fly him from pond to pond in search of insects and water plants.

He is puzzled by his big feet and makes a careful inspection.

Satisfied that all is well, he strides off in search of something to eat. He has mastered the art of using those long lily shoes and is proud of his skill.

"What's this?" He is disappointed to find only a dried piece of grass.

Suddenly comes danger. He is in the water where hungry eels lurk deep in the mud on the bottom of the pond.

His long legs and toes make it hard for him to climb back onto the leaf. But mother Lotus Bird has not lost sight of him.

She comes running to help her precious chick onto the leaf by pressing its edge into the water, making an aquatic ramp.

Full of concern she calls to him and encourages him onto the leaf. He is such a tiny mite and only the top of his head and his bill can be seen above the water.

Exhausted and miserable, baby Lotus Bird drags himself onto the safety of the leaf.

Weak and dripping wet he shelters gratefully under her open wing.

As she carries him back to the others he slowly slides away from under her.

His tiny wings appear dwarfed by his hanging feet.

He flops onto the leaf gasping but soon hurries towards his mother. The one place that he wants most to be is under her protective wing.

The other chicks have the same idea and they, too, seek shelter.

How comfortable and secure are the chicks under her wings! See their six legs and twenty-four toes?

Two weeks trotting over hundreds of lilies searching for food didn't make much difference to their body size but their bills and legs were an entirely different matter. The Lotus Bird family lived happily together on their lagoon — the chicks busy and beautiful and their mother proud and protective.

Solitude — that moment alone when soft light calls the mood and commands stillness.

Pied Oystercatcher

Pied Oystercatchers are striking examples of our numerous seashore and wading birds. They are decorated in black and white with vermilion bill and bright red eyes and legs. Oystercatchers are often seen in pairs feeding along sandy beaches or tidal mudflats and estuaries. During courtship and nesting the attractive pair run side by side cutting across each other's pathway and bowing together. They both share in incubating the eggs and caring for the young.

The effect of backlighting usually beautifies the world of nature. Notice the bill of the Oystercatcher glowing in early morning sunlight.

It took three days for this cute Oystercatcher chick to hatch after the first cracks appeared on the shell. All the "cheeps" and "whistles" from within were pleadings for release from this "prison house" of eggshell.

Dotterels

The Black-fronted Dotterel is common around the edges of lakes and swamps and is often observed running along the muddy edges and diluvial flats in search of insects and small creatures.

Dotterel eggs on the ground are well camouflaged and so are the young when hatched. Within an hour or two after birth they are up and running around with their parents.

Only a few hours old yet already decorated in camouflage-style sports-coats these Black-fronted Dotterel chicks remain montionless when danger approaches.

The Red-capped Dotterel enjoys life on sandy ocean shores and inland salt lakes. It is fascinating to watch the speed at which these small birds can run!

Spur-winged Plover

Spur-winged Plovers (now known as Masked Lapwings) increase in vocal activity during
rainy weather although their loud cackling calls may be heard at any time during the day
or night throughout the year. Both parent birds have a yellow black-tipped spur on each
wing and yellow wattles growing on the face. Plovers feed on insects and small
invertebrates but will eat seeds and vegetation during dry spells. The eggs are laid in a
shallow depression on the ground and blend in well with the undergrowth of chosen
surroundings.

These plover chicks are only a few hours old and beautifully decorated with sporty jackets, fluffy fronts and small wattles on the face. They can hide themselves well by lying flat amongst the grass and rough pasture.

Young plovers are quite active at night but must be ever alert for dangerous predators such as cats and foxes.

Seagull

Man has long gazed into azure space or misty ravine and envied these masters of thermal air currents.

Ibis

This sturdy bird is known as the farmers' friend. Ibises hunt with military precision stalking in line across a paddock stirring up grasshoppers with their feet and clearing them out in enormous numbers.

Pheasant Coucal

Australia has no native pheasants and the only resemblance to such birds is the Pheasant Coucal, commonly known as Swamp Pheasant, shown here drying out saturated feathers after searching for food in the long wet grass. Long tail feathers and wings display bar markings similar to birds of the cuckoo family. Coucals build domed nests in the long grass and raise strange looking black chicks covered in white, wiry down.

Plumed Egret

The graceful Plumed Egret is adorned with soft filamentary breeding feathers extending down the back and breast. These beautiful birds in past years were shot while on the nest for their magnificent plumes to decorate the hats of human beings! The baby egrets were callously left to starve in the nest.

Cute egret chicks have to change considerably before they can display the attractive style of their parents.

KINGFISHERS

Sacred Kingfisher

How fascinating is flight! Within one second the Sacred Kingfisher will slow from over forty kilometres per hour and alight at the entrance to the nesting tunnel.

The beautiful display of fanned tail and wings is almost too quick for the human eye to catch.

A superbly efficient three-point brake system neatly folds away as the landing gear contacts the bank.

Newly hatched kingfishers are blind and naked and look like something from another planet. The little chick on the right is concerned about the roof caving in and seems to be doing his best to hold everything up while his brothers flounder in their blind newness.

After six days of growing the eyes are about to open and there are signs of pin-feather development.

After several days of looking like nobody's children, turquoise blue and green feathers burst forth, providing beauty as well as warmth to the growing kingfishers.

The protective membrane which covers each eye from possible damage is clearly seen on the chick on the right. Water birds bring this safety membrane into use when feeding under water.

Azure Kingfisher

A shrill piercing note and blue flash reveal the kingfisher as it darts along the stream with food for the young.

After putting small fish, head first, into wide open baby mouths the kingfisher backs out, blasting away from the tunnel with sand and soil falling from the body and feet.

What a picture of absolute beauty as three young kingfishers enjoy their first day out of that tunnel in the bank and gaze at their colourful aquatic world.

Kookaburra

Most Laughing Kookaburras live in family groups and the young often stay with their parents for years, assisting with the raising of each new batch of hatchlings. They live mainly on a diet of insects and invertebrates but an interesting part of their feeding behaviour is the catching and killing of snakes. Kookaburras will sometimes tackle a snake that is almost too big and a tough battle is waged before their writhing, squirming prey is subdued.

This newly hatched kookaburra has been fed a small yellow-naped snake. He staggers beside the egg with the reptile stuck in his neck. He made valiant efforts to swallow the snake but was unequal to the task so his parents ate it themselves.

The second egg has hatched and the very new chick leans on his mate, with both showing signs of their exhausting birth struggle.

Even young kookaburras go through the embarrassing stages of adolescence but instead of pimples and blotches they have spikes and prickles!

Tawny Frogmouth

The Tawny Frogmouth belongs to the nightjar family of nocturnal birds and selects open forked branches upon which to build a simple flat nest, often lined with green leaves.

Soft oom-oom-oom notes reveal the presence of the Tawny Frogmouth in the dark of the night as it watches out for insects and small rodents.

This grey colour-phase Tawny Frogmouth has had a late day's night out and is trying to catch up on some sleep.

Most nocturnal birds display attractive patterns above and below the wings whilst in flight.

NIGHTLIFE

Lustrous white eggs show signs of cracking open after three weeks and the attractive hatchlings increase in beauty as they develop.

How proud Mr and Mrs Tawny must be of their beautiful twins with their wide open mouths, bright blue eyes and soft fluffy coats.

Young Tawny has left the nest and is all dressed up to go to town. It is dusk and the time has come to follow mum and dad to see how they catch all those insects in the dark.

White, heart-shaped face and black beady eyes give the Barn Owl considerable animation as he peers into car headlights at night. Barn Owl, also known as Delicate Owl, reveals symmetrical bar markings as he spreads his wings in a threat display.

To walk into a rainforest is to enter another world. Tall sturdy trees soaring th
forty metres up to the sunlight send light shafts down from their high leafy ca
to spotlight vines, creepers, orchids and ferns in the shade beneath. The rain
floor is a thick carpet of leaves, rich in food for birds and animals and for the
growth of plants both of beauty and of potential value to science and medicin

Moist conditions and ideal humidity accelerate the growth of fragile, colourful forms of fungi — beautiful examples of plant life existing without the usual photosynthesis process involving chlorophyll. Most colourful fungi have a visible root system called mycelium — tiny threads reaching out and forming a fine silk appearance.

Richest colours are seen in the youngest plants and as they grow there is often a slow change to softer tones.

Because of the wide variety of shapes and colours fungi are given many descriptive names. This attractive symmetrical form is commonly known as "Cup Fungus".

Many stems may grow from one base with cap-style heads neatly positioned beside each other.

Red Velvet Mites are common in the rainforest and these parasites belong to the Arachnid family: having eight legs — similar to ticks and spiders.

Of all the shapes and colours of these unusual plants Coral Fungi would surely be the most attractive, with colour varying from pure white to soft pink. Some of these plants may grow to 15cm in height and add special beauty to our magnificent rainforests.

Regent Bower Bird

The dazzling Regent Bower Bird is regarded as one of the most beautiful birds in the world. This striking bird with its contrasting yellow and black, and a touch of orange on its face, adds golden colour to the spectacular rainforests of eastern Australia.

At O'Reilly's Guest House, situated in the magnificent Lamington National Park, guests enjoy the unique experience of having these brilliant birds come to feed from the hand.

The male climbs up the side of the bower to re-arrange some of the twigs while the female watches intently.

His precious collection of old snail shells, cicada cases, leaves and berries is placed within the avenue of the bower. He excitedly goes through a courtship display, singing softly and offering her snail shells.

Courtship may last for five to ten minutes. Then he mates with her after dancing around to her end of the bower.

The young male Regent must wait a number of years before he can sport that rich coat of yellow and black but this does not deter him from building a bower and courting the female. His bill gradually turns yellow, revealing first signs of colour change.

After finding the bower of the young male the mature Regent spent some time courting and dancing before a female. He then destroyed the bower by pulling all the sticks out of the ground and taking the shells and berries to his own playground.

Female Regents build the nest, incubate the eggs and raise the young unassisted by the male, who spends most of his time tending his bower and courting other females. She builds the nest high in the rainforest trees in the shelter of thick growth and vines. The nest is a flimsy, saucer-shaped platform of thin twigs barely sufficient to hold the two attractively marked eggs.

Regent Bower Bird chicks display silver-grey coats and bright yellow mouths. Perhaps one of these beautiful young birds will one day grace our bushland with a flash of yellow and velvet-black — a sight to thrill all who are privileged to see it.

Glen Threlfo's strategy to take these unique photos was to catch march flies, wood cockroaches and small cicadas, delicacies to a Regent Bower Bird. He climbed again and again high up into the canopy to win mother Regent's confidence, but well before her babies hatched she had learned to take these tasty morsels from his shirt pocket and not to be disturbed by his camera.

During summer the many fruiting trees provide a wide variety of food but throughout winter food is scarce and Regent Bower Birds form bands — spending much time foraging in the lower altitude forests. Glen's patient watching is rewarded and his clever photography shows mother Regent's devotion at feeding time.

Satin Bower Bird

Resplendent blue feathers and vivid lilac blue eyes make the Satin Bower Bird a magnificent attraction of the bushland. His gleaming eyes bulge with excitement as he dances before his green and brown lady.

The male Satin takes a fancy to anything blue and places his collection around the bower. Wheezing, whirring rattles and buzzing notes, not unlike the worn-out starter motor of an old car, accompany the dancing and extraordinary display when the female approaches the playground.

At a distance King Satin Bower Bird's plumage looks plain black. Close up he is rich violet blue shot with various shades of violet and mauve. In his younger years his plumage was greenish like his mother's.

With great ideas of winning the heart of a lady the hopeful male Satin displays some of his precious possessions. When there are no blue man-made items in the locality the Satin Bower Bird collects blue feathers fallen from parrots, and blue or yellow flowers and berries, scattering them around the outside of the bower.

Even though the female is not as colour-saturated as the male her sapphire-blue eye is the centre of attraction. She is a devoted mother and has the sole responsibility of incubating the eggs and raising her hungry children.

 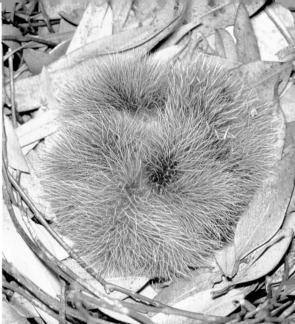

Young Satin Bower Birds are just like newborn babies — they are either crying out for food or sleeping. These two newly hatched chicks tuck their heads under their tummies and look like one grey, fluffy ball as they sleep and await the arrival of mum with more food.

At two weeks of age the chicks display their own distinction, quite oblivious that their father shows no interest in them and spends most of his time playing with his flowers, feathers and bits of plastic.

Albert's Lyrebird

Loud, rich notes on a cold winter morning reveal the presence of an Albert's Lyrebird as it highlights the dawn chorus in the misty sub-tropical rainforest. Rich rufous colours distinguish this splendid songster and mimic from the grey Superb Lyrebird.

The stately Albert's Lyrebird is confined to rainforests close to the eastern border separating Queensland and New South Wales. Instead of making a dancing mound on the ground this magnificent performer sometimes uses trampled vines on which to display and sing. The tail of the female is shorter and lacks the silver-grey filamentary and median feathers of her demonstrative mate.

It takes six weeks of incubation before the chick emerges from the blotched purple brown egg laid in a domed nest built between the buttresses of rainforest trees, on cliff faces or in the elkhorns and staghorns.

This timid little Lyrebird chick takes a peep at the wonderful green world outside and it will be many weeks before he leaves his warm, feather-lined home.

The gentle Albert's Lyrebird poses beside her fluffy chick — a picture of motherly love. These musicians and mimics of the rainforest are shy and wary, making descriptive photographs rare and valuable. Much time and energy were spent to obtain these pictures.

Lyrebird enters the nest to sit on her precious baby, her tail forming an awning at the entrance of the domed nest.

Little "Albie" comes out of the nest to stretch those long legs and show off his fancy football socks. He has spent six weeks sitting in the nest and looks forward to happy times roaming the rainforest with mum.

Eastern Yellow Robin

Eastern Yellow Robin introduces himself to your ear with loud chopping noises and soft piping calls. Your eye sees a flash of yellow in the mottled light of the rainforest, and you spy, in the foliage nearby, this charming little bird endeared of all who are in tune with nature's world.

King Parrot

Male King Parrot is a beautiful sight in and around eastern rainforests with his colour-saturated, dazzling orange-red breast and blue-green tail feathers.

Noisy Pitta

Noisy Pittas are gems of the rainforest sporting many colours of the spectrum. They spend most of their time hopping around the leafy floor searching for snails, insects and invertebrates. The young enjoy the shelter of the domed, mossy nest and express their impatience as both parents search diligently for food.

White-Browed Scrub Wrens

White-Browed Scrub Wrens spend most of their time on the ground searching for insects and their larvae. The young Scrub Wren has only recently left the nest and looks with amazement at the size of his meal. He almost chokes as he tries to swallow the dragonfly in one mouthful. But mother knows best and she stays to make certain that all goes down.

He has had enough and cannot take any more — even force-feed tactics are not working. But it won't be long before that closed mouth will be agape and uttering hungry cries for more food.

Eastern Spinebill

The beautiful Eastern Spinebill is often seen hovering in front of flowers and blossoms. The long, curved bill and exceptionally long tongue are designed to collect nectar from tubular flowers and cultivated fuchsias. Spinebills are likened to American hummingbirds because of their fast, erratic flight and their magnificent display of hovering.

The nest is skilfully
woven into the foliage
and is usually well
concealed. Pastel pink eggs
soon transform into cute
chicks with bright,
colourful mouths. Proud
father keeps a watchful eye
on his sleeping chick.

EDGE OF THE RAINFOREST

There is a magic strip of the bush where rainforest meets gum tree country — the sclerophyll. Insects abound so that food is plentiful for fantails, flycatchers and scores of other birds. From the cool, green depths again and again comes the crack of Whipbird's call. There is the harmony of Golden Whistler and Grey Thrush, the lament of Catbird and the incredible music and mimicry of Lyrebird. A harsher note comes from an Australian Bird of Paradise — Rifle Bird — and the loud protest of Satin Bower Bird disturbed at his bower. Tiny wrens flit and whisper in the undergrowth.

Move into the bright sunlight. Brilliant parrots fly over the eucalypts where honeyeaters feast on the nectar of the varied flowers and from the hillsides resounds the rich tuneful warble of magpies.

In a nearby tree flashes a touch of red from a Scarlet Robin.

Near his nest — a tunnel in a bank — is the gem-like sparkle of Spotted Pardalote — the Diamond bird.

Another sprightly flash of colour is friendly, nimble Superb Blue Wren.

In the rich grassland wallabies take their families for an airing. For those whose senses are awake, poetry wells up. Move back into the fragrant green tranquillity of the rainforest.

Regrowth

I know a place where dreams are born and time is never planned,
It cannot be found on any chart — for you must find it within your heart.

"Lord, your constant love reaches the heavens;
your faithfulness extends to the skies.
Your righteousness is towering like the mountains;
your justice is like the depths of the sea.
Men and animals are in your care.
How precious, O God, is your constant love!
We find protection under the shadow of your wings.
We feast on the abundant food you provide;
you let us drink from the river of your goodness.
You are the source of all life, and because of your light
we see the light."

King David
Psalm 36:5-9